BEADLE'S DIME SONG BOOK NO. 1

BEADLE'S DIME SONG BOOK NO. 1

VARIOUS

ISBN: 978-93-90294-83-1

Published: --

LECTOR HOUSE LLP
E-MAIL: lectorpublishing@gmail.com

BEADLE'S DIME SONG BOOK NO. 1

A COLLECTION OF NEW AND POPULAR COMIC AND SENTIMENTAL SONGS.

BY

VARIOUS

CONTENTS

Page

BEADLE'S DIME SONG BOOK.
NO. 1.

GENTLE ANNIE.

Thou wilt come no more, gentle Annie—
Like a flower thy spirit did depart;
Thou art gone, alas! like the many,
That have bloom'd in the summer of my heart.

CHORUS.

Shall we never more behold thee,
Never hear thy winning voice again,
When the spring time comes, gentle Annie,
When the wild flowers are scattered o'er the plain?

We have roam'd and loved 'mid the bowers,
When thy downy cheeks were in bloom;
Now I stand alone 'mid the flowers,
While they mingle their perfumes o'er thy tomb.
Chorus.—Shall we never more, &c.

Ah! the hours grow sad while I ponder
Near the silent spot where thou art laid,
And my heart bows down when I wander
By the streams and the meadows where we stray'd.
Chorus.—Shall we never more, &c.

NELLY GRAY.

There's a low green valley on the old Kentucky shore,
There I've whiled many happy hours away,
A sitting and a singing by the little cottage door
Where lived my darling Nelly Gray.

CHORUS.

Oh, my poor Nelly Gray, they have taken you away,
And I'll never see my darling any more,
I'm sitting by the river and I'm weeping all the day,
For you've gone from old Kentucky shore.

When the moon had climb'd the mountain, and the stars were shining too,
Then I'd take my darling Nelly Gray,
And we'd float down the river in my little light canoe—
While my banjo sweetly I would play.
Oh, my poor Nelly Gray, &c.

One night I went to see her, but she's gone, the neighbors say,
The white man bound her with his chain—
They have taken her to Georgia for to wear her life away,
As she toils in the cotton and the cane.
Oh, my poor Nelly Gray, &c.

My canoe is under water, and my banjo is unstrung,
I'm tired of living any more:
My eyes shall look downward, and my songs shall be unsung
While I stay on old Kentucky shore.
Oh, my poor Nelly Gray, &c.

My eyes are getting blinded and I can not see my way,
Hark! there's somebody knocking at the door:
Oh, I hear the angels calling, and I see my Nelly Gray;
Farewell to the old Kentucky shore.

CHORUS.

Oh, my Nelly Gray, up in heaven there they say
That they'll never take you from me any more:
I'm a coming, coming, coming, as the angels clear the way,

Farewell to the old Kentucky shore.

POOR OLD SLAVE.

Copied by permission of Russell & Tolman, 291 Washington St., Boston, owners of the copyright.

'Tis just one year ago to-day,
That I remember well,
I sat down by poor Nelly's side
A story she did tell;
'Twas about a poor, unhappy slave
That lived for many a year;
But now he's dead and in his grave,
No master does he fear.

Chorus. — The poor old slave has gone to rest,
We know that he is free;
Disturb him not, but let him rest,
Way down in Tennessee.

She took my arm, we walk'd along
Into an open field,
And here she paused to breathe awhile,
Then to his grave did steal.
She sat down by that little mound,
And softly whisper'd there,
"Come to me, father, 'tis thy child,"
Then gently dropp'd a tear.

Chorus. — The poor old slave, &c.

But since that time, how things have changed,
Poor Nelly that was my bride,
Is laid beneath the cold grave-sod,
With her father by her side.
I planted there upon her grave,
The weeping-willow tree,
I bathed its roots with many a tear,
That it might shelter me.

Chorus. — The poor old slave, &c.

A THOUSAND A YEAR.

Robin Ruff.—
If I had but a thousand a year, Gaffer Green—
If I had but a thousand a year,
What a man would I be, and what sights would I see,
If I had but a thousand a year.

Gaffer Green.—
The best wish you could have, take my word, Robin Ruff,
Would scarce find you, in bread or in beer;
But be honest and true, say what would you do,
If you had but a thousand a year.

Robin Ruff.—
I'd do—I scarcely know what, Gaffer Green,
I'd go—faith, I scarcely know where;
I'd scatter the chink, and leave others to think,
If I had but a thousand a year.

Gaffer Green.—
But when you are aged and gray, Robin Ruff,
And the day of your death it draws near,
Say, what with your pains, would you do with your gains
If you then had a thousand a year?

Robin Ruff.—
I scarcely can tell what you mean, Gaffer Green,
For your questions are always so queer;
But as other folks die, I suppose so must I,—
Gaffer Green.—
What! and give up your thousand a year?

There's a place that is better than this, Robin Ruff,—
And I hope in my heart you'll go there,—
Where the poor man's as great though he hath no estate,
Ay, as if he'd a thousand a year.

ANSWER TO A THOUSAND A YEAR.

Have you heard the strange news just come down, Gaffer Green,
That they're talking of now far and near?
How young Robin Ruff has his wish sure enough,
And he's now got a thousand a year, Gaffer Green!
He's now got a thousand a year!

Young Rob's a good heart, and I'm glad Master Cross,
Oh, it will not spoil him, never fear!
In the face of the poor he will not shut his door,
Though he has got a thousand a year, Master Cross!
Though he has got a thousand a year!

But 'twould be but the way of the world. Gaffer Green,
If he did not see *now* quite so clear;
They say *yellow* mists rise, and soon dim a man's eyes,
When he once gets a thousand a year, Gaffer Green!
When he once gets a thousand a year!

Robin's eyes were not dim t'other day, Master Cross,
When his poor old friend Harry was here;
Robin soon cured his pain, and soon made sunshine again,
With a touch of his thousand a year, Master Cross!
With a touch of his thousand a year!

Ah! but Rob must take care, must take care, Gaffer Green,
Or he'll spend all his new-gotten gear;
How much better 'twould be—he may want it, you see—
If he saved all his thousand a year, Gaffer Green!
If he saved all his thousand a year!

If he spends the last pound that he's got, Master Cross,
He'll be richer than some folks, I fear;
For a heart such as Rob's, though 'neath tatters it throbs,
Is worth ten times a thousand a year, Master Cross!
Is worth ten times a thousand a year!

THE OLD PLAY-GROUND.

I'm sitting to-day in the old play-ground,
Where you and I have sat so oft together,
I'm thinking of the joys when you and I were boys
In the merry days now gone, John, forever;
'Twas here we sat in the merry olden time,
And we dream'd of the wild world before us,
And our visions and hopes of the coming time
Were as bright as the sun that shone o'er us.

CHORUS.

I'm sitting to-day in the old play-ground,
Where you and I have sat so oft together,
I'm thinking of the joys when you and I were boys
In those merry days now gone, John, forever.

O'er the threshold, John, we pass'd forlorn,
To wander we knew not where,
The heaven we thought so bright was o'ershadow'd by night,
And the pathway lay dark and drear.
But I am sitting to-day in the old play-ground,
Where you and I have sat so oft together,
And these memories wild have made me a child,
As in the merry days now gone, John, forever.
CHORUS.—I'm sitting to-day, &c.

KITTY CLYDE.

Oh, who has not seen Kitty Clyde?
She lives at the foot of the hill,
In a sly little nook by the babbling brook,
That carries her father's old mill.
Oh, who does not love Kitty Clyde?
That sunny eyed, rosy cheek'd lass,
With a sweet dimpled chin that looks roguish as sin,
With always a smile as you pass.

CHORUS.

Sweet Kitty, dear Kitty, my own sweet Kitty Clyde,
In a sly little nook by the babbling brook,
Lives my own sweet Kitty Clyde.

With a basket to put in her fish,
Every morn with a line and a hook,
This sweet little lass, through the tall heavy grass,
Steals along by the clear running brook.
She throws her line into the stream,
And trips it along the brook side,
Oh, how I do wish that I was a fish.
To be caught by sweet Kitty Clyde.

Sweet Kitty, dear Kitty, &c.

How I wish that I was a Bee,
I'd not gather honey from flowers,
But would steal a dear sip from Kitty's sweet lip,
And make my own *hive* in her bowers.
Or, if I was some little bird,
I would not build nests in the air,
But keep close by the side of sweet Kitty Clyde,
And sleep in her soft silken hair,
Sweet Kitty, dear Kitty, &c.

WILLIE, WE HAVE MISSED YOU.

Oh! Willie, is it you, dear, safe, safe at home?
They did not tell me true, dear, they said you would not come,
I heard you at the gate, and it made my heart rejoice,
For I knew that welcome footstep, and that dear familiar voice,
Making music on my ear in the lonely midnight gloom,
Oh! Willie, we have miss'd you; welcome, welcome home.

We've long'd to see you nightly, but this night of all;
The fire was blazing brightly, and lights were in the hall,
The little ones were up 'till 'twas ten o'clock and past,
Then their eyes began to twinkle and they have gone to sleep at last;
But they listen'd for your voice till they thought you'd never come,
Oh! Willie, we have miss'd you; welcome, welcome home.

The days were sad without you, the nights long and drear,
My dreams have been about you, oh, welcome, Willie dear,
Last night I wept and watch'd, by the moonlight's cheerless ray,
Till I thought I heard your footsteps, then I wiped my tears away,
But my heart grew sad again, when I found you had not come;
Oh! Willie, we have missed you; welcome, welcome home.

WILLIE'LL ROAM NO MORE.

Yes, Mary, I have come, love, across the dark, blue sea,
To our peaceful, quiet home, love, our little ones and thee;
I've watch'd and waited nightly for the welcome hour to come,
When happily and brightly all the dear delights of home
Should greet my listening ear, love, upon my native shore;
Then wipe away thy tears, Mary, for thy Willie'll roam no more.

CHORUS.

Thy Willie'll roam no more, thy Willie'll roam no more,
Then wipe away thy tears, Mary, for thy Willie'll roam no more.

How often since I left you, love, in solitude and tears,
Have I bless'd that love which clung to me through many changing
years;
And while I paced the silent deck, forgotten and alone,
Has my heart recall'd thy love-lit smile, thy sweet and gentle tone.
Thy image, love, has e'er been shrined within this fond heart's core;
But wipe away thy tears, Mary, for thy Willie'll roam no more.

Chorus. — Thy Willie'll roam no more, &c.

Dear Mary, when in life's sweet morn, in all thy youthful pride,
I bore thee, virgin, bathed in tears, from thy fond mother's side,
And promised at the altar to love through life as now,
Say, Mary, when life's sorrows came, did I forget that vow?
Your heart will own I left you, love, our fortunes to restore;
Then wipe away thy tears, Mary, for thy Willie'll roam no more.

Chorus. — Thy Willie'll roam no more, &c.

KISS ME QUICK AND GO.

The other night while I was sparking
Sweet Turlina Spray,
The more we whisper'd our love talking,
The more we had to say;
The old folks and the little folks
We thought were fast in bed, —
We heard a footstep on the stairs,
And what d'ye think she said?

CHORUS.

"Oh! kiss me quick and go my honey,
Kiss me quick and go!
To cheat surprise and prying eyes,
Why kiss me quick and go!"

Soon after that I gave my love
A moonlight promenade,
At last we fetch'd up to the door
Just where the old folks stay'd;
The clock struck twelve, her heart struck two (too).
And peeping over head
We saw a night-cap raise the blind,
And what d'ye think she said?
Oh! kiss me quick and go my honey, &c.

One Sunday night we sat together,
Sighing side by side,
Just like two wilted leaves of cabbage
In the sunshine fried;
My heart with love was nigh to split
To ask her for to wed,
Said I: "Shall I go for the priest,"
And what d'ye think she said?
Oh! kiss me quick and go my honey, &c.

ANNIE LAURIE.

Maxwelton Braes are bonnie,
Where early fa's the dew,
And it's there that Annie Laurie
Gie'd me her promise true;
Gie'd me her promise true,
Which ne'er forget will be;
And for bonnie Annie Laurie
I'd lay me doune and dee.

Her brow is like the snaw-drift—
Her throat is like the swan,
Her face it is the fairest
That e'er the sun shone on—
That e'er the sun shone on—
And dark blue is her e'e;
And for bonnie Annie Laurie
I'd lay me doune and dee.

Like dew on the gowan lying,
Is the fa' o' her fairy feet,
And like the winds in summer sighing,
Her voice is low and sweet,
Her voice is low and sweet,
And she's a' the world to me;
And for bonnie Annie Laurie
I'd lay me doune and dee.

NELLY WAS A LADY.

Down on de Mississippi floating,
Long time I trabble on de way
All night de cotton-wood a toting,
Sing for my true lub all de day.

CHORUS.

Nelly was a lady,
Last night she died;
Toll de bell for lubly Nell,
My dark Virginny bride.

Now I'm unhappy and I'm weeping,
Can't tote de cotton-wood no more:
Last night, while Nelly was a sleeping,
Death came a knocking at de door.
Nelly was a lady, &c.

When I saw my Nelly in de morning
Smile till she open'd up her eyes,
Seem'd like de light ob day a dawning
Jist for de sun begin to rise.
Nelly was a lady, &c.

Close by de margin ob de water,
Whar de lone weeping-willow grows
Dar lib'd Virginny's lubly daughter,
Dar she in death may find repose.
Nelly was a lady, &c.

Down in de meadow 'mong the clober,
Walk wid my Nelly by my side:
Now all dem happy days am ober, —
Farewell, my dark Virginny bride,
Nelly was a lady, &c.

DOWN THE RIVER.

Oh! the river is up, and the channel is deep,
And the wind blows steady and strong;
Let the splash of your oars the measure keep,
As we row the old boat along.
Oh! the water is bright, and flashing like gold,
In the ray of the morning sun,
And old Dinah's away up out of the cold,
A getting the hoe-cake done.
Oh! the river is up, and the channel is deep,
And the wind blows steady and strong;
Let the splash of your oars the measure keep,
As we row the old boat along.

Chorus. — Down the river, down the river,
Down the Ohio;
Down the river, down the river,
Down the Ohio.

Chorus repeated.

Oh! the master is proud of the old broad-horn,
For it brings him plenty of tin;
Oh! the crew they are darkies, the cargo is corn,
And the money comes tumbling in.
There is plenty on board for the darkies to eat,
And there's something to drink and to smoke;
There's the banjo, the bones, and the tambourine,
There's the song, and the comical joke.
Oh! the river is up, and the channel is deep,
And the wind blows steady and strong;
Let the splash of your oars the measure keep,
As we row the old boat along.

Chorus. — Down the river, &c.

HAVE YOU SEEN MY SISTER?

Say, my lovely friends, have you any pity
At your finger-ends? then listen to my ditty.
Our Kate has gone away, last Thursday night we miss'd her;
Good people do not smile, — say, Have you seen my sister?

If you have her seen, I hope you will advise her
To return to me, or I must advertise her;
Her waist is very thick, her stays give her a twister,
Now tell me, b'hoys and g'hals, Have you seen my sister?

She squints with both her eyes, in a manner very shocking,
She's got a mouth for pies, and wears no shoes or stockings;
I'm afraid she's gone astray, and some chap did enlist her,
I'm afraid she's gone for good; say, Have you seen my sister?

She wants her two front teeth, you'd see it when she'd titter.
She's got such little feet, Victoria's shoes won't fit her;
She wears no cap at all, but a great big muslin whister,
Now tell me once for all, Have you seen my sister?

Her figure's straight and tall, her conduct's very proper;
She's well provided, for she's eighteen pence in copper.
Now if you have her seen, you never could forget her,
For she's very much like me; now, Have you seen my sister?

Her mouth is very small, her nose is straight and natty,
I tell you once for all, this girl is very pretty
Now I'll sing you another song, and it shall be a twister,
If you will go with me, and help me find my sister.

BOB RIDLEY.

Now white folks I'll sing you a ditty,
I'se from home, but dat's no pity,
Oh, to praise myself it am a shame,
But Robert Ridley is my name.

CHORUS.

Oh, Bob Ridley ho, Oh, Bob Ridley ho,
Oh, Bob Ridley! Oh! Oh!! Oh!!!
ROBERT RIDLEY HO!

Oh, white folks I hab cross'd de mountains
How many miles I didn't count 'em,
Oh, I'se left de folks at de old plantation
An' come down here for my edecation.
Oh, Bob Ridley ho, &c.

De first time dat I eber got a licken,
'Twas down at de forks ob de cotton picken;
Oh! it made me dance, it made me tremble,
I golly, it made my eyeballs jingle.
Oh, Bob Ridley ho, &c.

New York City am a mighty fine one,
For beauty and location it ain't behind none;
Oh! de ladies all look so sweet and gidley,
Wonder dey don't fall in love wid old Bob Ridley.
Oh, Bob Ridley ho, &c.

KATE KEARNEY.

Oh! did you ne'er hear of Kate Kearney?
She lives on the banks of Killarney:
From the glance of her eye, shun danger and fly,
For fatal's the glance of Kate Kearney.
For that eye is so modestly beaming,
You ne'er think of mischief she's dreaming;
Yet, oh! I can tell, how fatal's the spell,
That lurks in the eye of Kate Kearney.

O should you e'er meet this Kate Kearnev,
Who lives on the bank of Killarney,
Beware of her smile, for many a wile
Lies hid in the smile of Kate Kearney.
Though she looks so bewitchingly simple,
Yet there's mischief in every dimple;
And who dares inhale her sigh's spicy gale,
Must die by the breath of Kate Kearney.

ANSWER TO KATE KEARNEY.

Oh, yes, I have seen this Kate Kearney,
Who lives near the lake of Killarney;
From her love-beaming eye, what mortal can fly,
Unsubdued by the glance of Kate Kearney?
For that eye so seducingly meaning,
Assures me of mischief she's dreaming;
And I feel 'tis in vain to fly from the chain
That binds me to lovely Kate Kearney.

At eve when I've met this Kate Kearney,
On the flower-mantled banks of Killarney,
Her smile would impart thrilling joy to my heart,
As I gaz'd on the charming Kate Kearney.
On the banks of Killarney reclining,
My bosom to rapture resigning,
I've felt the keen smart of love's fatal dart,
And inhal'd the warm sigh of Kate Kearney.

HOME AGAIN.

Home again, home again,
From a foreign shore;
And, oh, it fills my soul with joy,
To meet my friends once more
Here I dropp'd the parting tear,
To cross the ocean's foam;
But now I'm once again with those
Who kindly greet me home.
Home again, &c.

Happy hearts, happy hearts,
With mine have laugh'd in glee,
But, oh, the friends I loved in youth
Seem happier to me.
And if my guide should be the fate
Which bids me longer roam,
But death alone can break the tie
That binds my heart to home
Home again, &c.

Music sweet, music soft,
Lingers round the place;
And, oh, I feel the childhood charm,
That time can not afface.
Then give me but my homestead roof,
I'll ask no palace dome;
For I can live a happy life
With those I love at home.
Home again, &c.

GENTLE JENNIE GRAY.

My heart is sad, I'll tell you why,
If you'll listen to my lay,
Which makes me weep, when I sing
Of my gentle Jennie Gray;
But I never can forget the days,
When with Jennie by my side,
We talk'd of love and happiness,
When she should be my bride.

Chorus.—Hush the banjo, toll the bell,
I'm very sad to-day,
I can not work, so let me weep,
For my gentle Jennie Gray.

My Jennie had the sweetest face,
And eyes of sparkling jet,
With lips like new-born roses,
She was my darling pet;
But Death he called one morning,
And took my love away,
And left me lonely weeping,
For my gentle Jennie Gray.

Chorus.—Hush the banjo, &c.

And in the ground they laid her,
Close by my cabin door;
A rude stone marks the spot,
Where she sleeps to wake no more;
While at her grave I'm weeping,
At every close of day,
I fancy then, she's sleeping,
And not dead! my Jennie Gray.

Chorus.—Hush the banjo, &c.

FADED FLOWERS.

Copied by permission of Russell & Tolman, 291 Washington St., Boston, owners
of the copyright.

The flowers I saw in the wild wood,
Have since dropp'd their beautiful leaves,
And the many dear friends of my childhood,
Have slumber'd for years in their graves;
But the bloom of the flowers I remember,
Though their smiles I shall never more see,
For the cold, chilly winds of December
Stole my flowers, my companions, from me.

The roses may bloom on the morrow,
And many dear friends I have won,
But my heart can part with but sorrow,
When I think of the ones that are gone.
'Tis no wonder that I am broken-heart'd
And stricken with sorrow should be,
For we have met, we have loved, we have part'd,
My flowers, my companions, and me.

How dark looks this world, and how dreary,
When we part from the ones that we love,
But there's rest for the faint and the weary,
And friends meet with lost ones above;
But in heaven I can but remember,
When from earth my proud soul shall be free,
That no chilly winds of December,
Shall steal my companions from me.

HARD TIMES.

Listen awhile and give ear to my song
Concerning these hard times, 'twill not take you long,
How every one tries each other to bite,
And in cheating each other they think they do right.
Nothing but hard times.

There are some young men, which you very well know,
To see pretty girls they are sure to go;
The old folks will giggle, they will laugh, and they'll grin,
Crying, "Use him well, Sal, or he'll not come again."

The baker will cheat you in the bread that you eat,
And so will the butcher, in the weight of his meat;
He'll tip up the steelyards, and make them go down,
And swears it is weight, when it lacks a half pound.

The next are the ladies, the sweet little dears,
At the balls and the parties, how nice they appear;
With whalebones and corsets themselves they will squeeze,
You have to unlace them before they can sneeze.

Next is the tinker, he'll mend all your ware,
For little or nothing, some ale or some beer;
But before he begins, he'll get half drunk or more,
And in stopping one hole, why he'll punch twenty more.

The judge on his bench, so honest and true,
He'll stare at a man, as though he'd look him through;
He'll send him a year or six months to the jail,
And for five dollars more, why he'll go your bail.

Then next is the doctor, he'll cure all your ills,
With his puffs and his powders, his syrups, and squills,
He'll give you a dose that will make you grow fat,
Or some pills that will leave you but your boots and your hat.

The ladies must all have their silks and their laces,
And things they call bonnets, to show off their faces;
But their figure, however, can never be seen,
For they are hoop'd like a barrel, with French crinoline.

The last is the sheriff, who thinks himself wise,
He'll come to your house with a big pack of lies;

He'll take all your property that he can sell,
And get drunk on the money, that's doing right well,
In these hard times.

BEN BOLT.

Don't you remember sweet Alice, Ben Bolt?
Sweet Alice, with hair so brown,
Who blush'd with delight if you gave her a smile,
And trembled with fear at your frown?
In the old church-yard in the valley, Ben Bolt,
In a corner obscure and lone,
They have fitted a slab of granite so gray,
And Alice lies under the stone.

Under the hickory tree, Ben Bolt,
That stood at the foot of the hill,
Together we've lain in the noonday shade,
And listen'd to Appleton's mill.
The mill-wheel has fallen to pieces, Ben Bolt,
The rafters have tumbled in,
And a quiet that crawls round the wall as you gaze,
Takes the place of the olden din.

Do you mind the cabin of logs, Ben Bolt,
That stood in the pathless wood?
And the button-ball tree with its motley boughs,
That nigh by the door-step stood?
The cabin to ruin has gone, Ben Bolt,
You would look for the tree in vain;
And where once the lords of the forest stood,
Grows grass and the golden grain.

And don't you remember the school, Ben Bolt,
And the master, so cruel and grim?
And the shady nook in the running brook,
Where the children went to swim?
Grass grows on the master's grave, Ben Bolt—
The spring of the brook is dry;
And of all the boys who were school-mates then
There are only you and I!

There's a change in the things I love, Ben Bolt?
They have changed from the old to the new;

But I feel in the core of my spirit the truth,
There never was a change in you.
Twelvemonths twenty have pass'd, Ben Bolt,
Since first we were friends, yet I hail
Thy presence a blessing, thy friendship a truth,
Ben Bolt of the salt-sea gale!

POOR JUNEY.

Pearl River's side is far away, in Mississippi State,
Where our Old Cabin stands alone, with Juney at the gate;
I told her I was going away, but would not stay out late,
And so she thought I'd soon be home, and waited at the gate.

CHORUS

The Cabin stands upon the stream in Mississippi State,
And I must quickly hurry home and take her from the gate.

Old Massa died, and I was sold away to Georgia's State,
They did not buy my sister Jane when they bought me her mate,
I could not tell her we must part, alas! our cruel fate,
And so, with weeping eyes, she stands to meet me at the gate.
The Cabin stands upon the stream, &c.

I can't forget her gloomy look, when I bid her good-night,
Nor how my body quaked and shook as slow I left her sight;
But soon I'll gold and silver get, pray Heaven I'm not too late,
To buy my darling Juney free and take her from the gate.
The Cabin stands upon the stream, &c.

Oh, Juney was a simple child, with pretty shining curls,
And white folks loved her best of all, the young Mulatto girl,
'Twas wrong for me to leave her 'lone, in Mississippi State,
But money it shall break the chain that binds her to the gate.
The Cabin stands upon the stream, &c.

If you go away down South, to Mississippi State,
Don't fail to seek our Cabin there, with Juney at the gate;
Tell her to wait a little while, tell her in hope to wait,
For I am he shall make her free, and take her from the gate.
The Cabin stands upon the stream, &c.

THE LITTLE BLACKSMITH.

We heard his hammer all day long
On the anvil ring, and ring,
But he always came when the sun went down,
To sit on the gate and sing;
His little hands so hard and brown
Cross'd idly on his knee,
And straw-hat lopping over cheeks
As red as they could be.

Chorus. —The hammer's stroke on the anvil, fill'd
His heart with a happy ring,
And that was why, when the sun went down,
He came to the gate to sing.

His blue and faded jacket, trimm'd
With signs of work, his feet
All bare and fair upon the grass,
He made a picture sweet.
For still his shoes, with iron shod,
On the smithy wall he hung,
As forth he came, when the sun went down,
And sat on the gate and sung.

Chorus. —The hammer's stroke on the anvil, fill'd, &c.

The whistling rustic tending cows,
Would keep in pastures near,
And half the busy villagers
Lean from their doors to hear.
And from the time the robin came
And made the hedges bright,
Until the stubble yellow grew,
He never miss'd a night.

Chorus. —The hammer's stroke on the anvil, &c.

OVER THE MOUNTAIN.

Over the mountain wave,
See where they come;
Storm cloud and wintry wind
Welcome them home;
Yet where the sounding gale
Howls to the sea,
There their song peals along
Deep-toned and free.

Chorus.—Pilgrims and wanderers.
Hither we come;
Where the free dare to be,
This is our home.

England hath sunny dales,
Dearly they bloom;
Scotia hath heather hills,
Sweet their perfume;
Yet through the wilderness
Cheerful we stray,
Native land, native land,
Home far away!

Chorus.—Pilgrims and wanderers, &c.

Dim grew the forest path,
Onward they trod;
Firm beat their noble hearts,
Trusting in God;
Gray men and blooming maids,
High rose their song,
Hear it sweep clear and deep,
Ever along.

Chorus.—Pilgrims and wanderers, &c.

Not theirs the glory wreath
Torn by the blast;
Heavenward their holy steps,
Heavenward they pass'd;
Green be their mossy graves,

Ours be their fame,
While their song peals along
Ever the same.
Chorus. —Pilgrims and wanderers, &c.

ROW, ROW.

Row! row! homeward we steer,
Twilight falls o'er us,
Hark! hark! music is near,
Friends glide before us,
Song lightens our labor,
Sing as onward we go,
Keep each with his neighbor
Time as we flow.

Chorus. —Row! row! homeward we go,
Twilight falls o'er us,
Row! row! sing as we flow,
Day flies before us.

Row! row! sing as we go,
Nature rejoices;
Hark! how the hills as we flow
Echo our voices;
Still o'er the dark waters
Far away we must roam,
Ere Italy's daughters
Welcome us home.

Chorus. —Row! row, &c.

Row! row! see in the west
Lights dimly burning,
Friends in yon harbor of rest
Wait our returning;
See now they burn clearer, —
Keep time with the oar;
Now, now we are nearer
That happy shore.

Chorus. —Row! row, &c.

Home, home, daylight is o'er,
Friends stand before us;
Yet ere our boat touch the shore,
Once more the chorus.

Chorus. —Row! row, &c.

THE MILLER OF THE DEE.

There dwelt a miller hale and bold
Beside the river Dee;
He work'd and sang from morn till night,
No lark more blithe than he;
And this, the burden of his song,
Forever used to be,
"I envy nobody, no, not I,
And nobody envies me."

"Thou'rt wrong my friend," said old King Hal,
"Thou'rt wrong as wrong can be;
For could my heart be light as thine,
I'd gladly change with thee;
And tell me now what makes thee sing
With voice so loud and free,
While I am sad, though I am King
Beside the river Dee."

The miller smiled, and doff'd his cap,
"I earn my bread," quoth he
"I love my wife, I love my friends,
I love my children three;
I owe no penny I can not pay,
I thank the river Dee,
That turns the mill, that grinds the corn
To feed my babes and me."

"Good friend," said Hal, and sigh'd the while,
"Farewell and happy be;
But say no more, if thou'dst be true,
That no one envies thee;
Thy mealy cap is worth my crown,
Thy mill my kingdom's fee,
Such men as thou are England's boast,
Oh, miller of the Dee."

ALL'S FOR THE BEST.

All's for the best! be sanguine and cheerful;
Trouble and sorrow are friends in disguise,
Nothing but folly goes faithless and fearing,
Courage forever! is happy and wise.
All's for the best! if a man would but know it,
Providence wishes that all may be blest,
This is no dream of the pundit or poet,
Fact is not fancy, and all's for the best!

Chorus.—All's for the best! All's for the best!
Fact is not fancy, and all's for the best.

All's for the best: set this on your standard,
Soldier of sadness, or pilgrim of love,
Who to the shores of despair may have wander'd
A way-wearied swallow, or heart-stricken dove.
All's for the best! be a man, but confiding,
Providence tenderly governs the rest,
And the frail bark of his creature is guiding
Wisely and warily, all's for the best!

Chorus.—All's for the best, &c,

All's for the best dispel idle terrors,
Meet all your fears and your foes in the van,
And in the midst of your dangers and errors,
Trust like a child, and strive like a man.
All's for the best! unfailing, unbounded,
Providence wishes that all may be blest,
And both by wisdom and mercy surrounded,
Hope and be happy, then all's for the best!

Chorus.—All's for the best! All's for the best!
Hope and be happy, then all's for the best.

DON'T BE ANGRY MOTHER.

Don't be angry mother, mother,
Let thy smiles be smiles of joy,
Don't be angry, mother, mother,
Don't be angry with thy boy.
Years have flown since we have travers'd
The dark and stormy sea;
Whilst your boy quite broken-heart'd,
Ne'er has ceased to think of thee.

Don't be angry mother, mother,
Let the world say what it will,
Though I don't deserve thy favor,
Yet I fondly love thee still;
We have lived and loved together,
And our hearts ne'er knew a pain
But forgive me, mother, mother,
Oh, forgive thy boy again.

Pray, remember, mother, mother,
I've been kneeling at thy feet,
And I am dreaming of thee nightly,
While reclining in my sleep;
But forgive me, mother, mother,
It will ease thy heart of pain,
But forgive me, mother, mother,
Oh, forgive thy boy again.

I AM NOT ANGRY.

I am not angry, dearest boy,
No cloud is on my brow,
Thou seest only smiles of joy,
I am not angry now.
A mother's heart has yearn'd for thee,
A mother's tears have flown,
A mother's prayers been offer'd up
To the eternal throne:
And though thou hast been wayward, boy,
Misguided by thy will,
A mother's love is thine, my boy
Thou art my darling still.

While thou wert on the rolling deep,
Toss'd by the rugged sea,
My only comfort was to weep—
To weep and pray for thee.
Over thy follies I have shed,
Ah! many a bitter tear,
And I have mourn'd for thee as dead
Through all the passing year;
Yet I have pray'd that thou, my son,
Might'st catch my latest breath,
That thy dear hands, and thine alone,
Might close my eyes in death.

I do forgive thee now, my boy,
It frees my heart from pain,
My bosom throbs alone with joy
To see thy face again.
Though thou hast wander'd far from me,
I'll yet forgive the past,
For I am happy, boy, to see
Thou hast return'd at last.
Yes, now this heart is fill'd with joy,
My sororws are all o'er,
For thou art here again, my boy,
And we shall part no more.

MY HOME IN KENTUCK.

I long, how I long for my home in Kentuck,
With its fields where I labor'd, so green,
Where the possum and the coon, and the juicy wild duck,
And the 'bacco so prime, I have seen:
There I've fish'd from the banks of the Masella creek,
And oft, in the shades of the night,
Have I watch'd with my gun, nigh the old Salt Lick,
For the game as it come to my sight.

Chorus.—There is my old cabin home,
There are my sisters and brother,
There is my wife, joy of my life,
My child, and the grave of my mother.

That hut, my dear home, my log-cabin home,
With the bench that I stood at the door,
Where weary at night, from my work I would come
And there rest, ere I stepp'd on its floor.
The calabash vine, that then clung to its walls,
Oh! 'tis dear in my memory still to me,
And my master, who lives in his own handsome halls,
Not so happy as then I could be.

Chorus.—There is my old cabin home, &c.

But that cabin is far, far away from me now,
I am far from the scenes that I love,
Far away from that wife who once heard me vow
That forever I faithful would prove—
My friends are still there, and still there is my child,
And still there, all in life, I must crave—
Still there is that mound, with its flowers so wild,
That covers my old mother's grave,
Chorus.—There is my old cabin home, &c.

DO THEY MISS ME AT HOME.

Do they miss me at home, do they miss me!
'Twould be an assurance most dear,
To know that this moment some loved one,
Were saying I wish he was here,
To feel that the group at the fireside
Were thinking of me as I roam,
Oh, yes, 'twould be joy beyond measure
To know that they miss'd me at home,
To know that they miss'd me at home.

When twilight approaches, the season
That ever is sacred to song,
Does some one repeat my name over,
And sigh that I tarry so long?
And is there a chord in the music
That's miss'd when my voice is away,
And a chord in each heart that awaketh
Regret at my wearisome stay,
Regret at my wearisome stay.

Do they sit me a chair near the table,
When evening's home pleasures are nigh,
When the candles are lit in the parlor,
And the stars in the calm azure sky?
And when the "good-nights" are repeated,
And all lay them down to their sleep,
Do they think of the absent, and waft me
A whisper'd "good-night" while they weep,
A whisper'd "good-night" while they weep?

Do they miss me at home—do they miss me
At morning, at noon, or at night?
And lingers one gloomy shade round them
That only my presence can light?
Are joys less invitingly welcome,
And pleasures less hale than before,
Because one is miss'd from the circle,
Because I am with them no more,
Because I am with them no more!

UNFURL THE GLORIOUS BANNER.

Unfurl the glorious banner, let it sway upon the breeze,
The emblem of our country's pride, on land, and on the seas
The emblem of our liberty, borne proudly in the wars,
The hope of every freeman, the gleaming stripes and stars.

CHORUS.

Then unfurl the glorious banner out upon the welcoming air,
Read the record of the olden time upon its radiance there;
In the battle it shall lead us, and our banner ever be,
A beacon-light to glory, and a guide to victory.

The glorious band of patriots who gave the flag its birth,
Have writ with steel in history, the record of its worth;
From east to west, from sea to sea, from pole to tropic sun,
Will eyes grow bright, and hearts throb high at the name of Washington.

Chorus.—Then unfurl the glorious banner, &c.

Ah! proudly should we bear it, and guard this flag of ours,
Borne bravely in its infancy amidst the darker hours;
Only the brave may bear it, a guardian it shall be
For those who well have won the right to boast of liberty.

Chorus.—Then unfurl the glorious banner, &c.

The meteor flag of seventy-six, long may it wave in pride,
To tell the world how nobly the patriot fathers died:
When from the shadows of their night outburst the brilliant sun,
It bathed in light the stripes and stars, and lo! the field was won.

Chorus.—Then unfurl the glorious banner, &c.

MY OWN NATIVE LAND

I've roved over mountain, I've cross'd over flood;
I've traversed the wave-rolling sand;
Though the fields were as green, and the moon shone as bright,
Yet it was not my own native land.
No, no, no, no, no, no. No, no, no, no, no, no,
Though the fields were as green, and the moon shone as bright,
Yet it was not my own native land.

The right hand of friendship how oft I have grasp'd
And bright eyes have smiled and looked bland,
Yet happier far were the hours that I pass'd
In the West—in my own native land.
Yes, yes, yes, yes, yes, yes. Yes, yes, yes, yes, yes, yes,
Yet happier far were the hours that I pass'd
In the West—in my own native land.

Then hail, dear Columbia, the land that we love,
Where flourishes Liberty's tree;
The birth-place of Freedom, our own native home,
'Tis the land, 'tis the land of the free!
Yes, yes, yes, yes, yes, yes. Yes, yes, yes, yes, yes, yes,
The birth-place of Freedom, our own native home,
'Tis the land, 'tis the land of the free!

ROOT HOG OR DIE.

I'll tell you of a story that happened long ago,
When the English came to America, I s'pose you all do know,
They couldn't whip the Yankees, I'll tell you the reason why,
Uncle Sam made 'em sing, Root Hog or Die.

John Bull sent to Boston, as you shall plainly see,
Forty large ships loaded clear up with tea;
The Yankees wouldn't pay the tax, I'll tell the reason why,
The Yankee boys made em sing, Root Hog or Die,

They first met our armies on the top of Bunker Hill,
When it came to fighting, I guess they got their fill;
The Yankee boys chased them off, I'll tell you the reason why,
The Yankee boys made 'em sing, Root Hog or Die.

Then they met our Washington at Yorktown,
There the Yankees mow'd 'em down, like grass from the ground;
Old Cornwallis gave up his sword, I'll tell you the reason why,
General Washington made 'em sing, Root Hog or Die.

Then they came to Baltimore forty years ago,
They tried to take North Point, but found it wouldn't go;
The Baltimoreans chased them off, I'll tell the reason why
The Yankee boys made 'em sing Root Hog or Die.

Then they march'd their arms down to New Orleans,
That was the place, I think, that Jackson gave 'em beans;
They couldn't take our cotton bales, I'll tell the reason why,
General Jackson made 'em sing, Root Hog or Die.

Now Johnny Bull has been kicking up a fuss,
He'd better keep quiet or he'll surely make it worse,
We're bound to have Cuba, I'll tell you the reason why,
For Uncle Sam will make 'em sing, Root Hog or Die.

ROOT HOG OR DIE, NO. 2.

The greatest old nigger that ever I did see,
Look'd like a sick monkey up a sour apple-tree;
It don't make a bit of difference to either you or I
Big pig, little pig, root hog or die.

CHORUS.

Chief cook and bottle washer, captain of the waiters,
Stand upon your head while you peel a bag of taters.
Jog along.

I come from old Virginny with a pocket-full of news
I am worth four shillings, standing in my shoes;
Doesn't make a bit of difference to either you or I,
Little pig, big pig, root hog or die.
Chief cook, &c.

The Broadway niggers look so mighty grand,
Shanghai coats and gloves upon the hand,
A big standing collar, standing away up to the sky,
Little pig, big pig, root hog or die.
Chief cook, &c.

Oh, these Broadway gals look so mighty gay,
With their hoop'd skirts promenading Broadway,
Their bonnets on their shoulders, and their noses to the sky,
They go it in the sun or shade—root hog or die.
Chief cook, &c.

ROOT HOG OR DIE, NO. 3.

I am a jolly nigger as ever you did see,
I come from Alabama just for to have a spree;
I tought I come to York, dey do things up so high,
Bound to have a spree, boys—root hog or die.

CHORUS.

New York gals—dey are so mighty tender,
Have to put on hoops when dey go out on a bender.
Jog along.

I jump'd upon de boat as she started from de lebby,
Dey put me in de hole in something of a hurry,
De coal dey made me shovel, oh, how dey made me fly;
Dat's de way I come, boys—root hog or die.
New York gals, &c.

You tallk about your niggers dat grow up in de North,
Can't compete wid dis one dat sprouted in de South,
Dey call me Blind Dick, kase I've only got one eye,
Dat's not my name, boys—root hog or die.
New York gals, &c.

When I take a walk I look so mighty gay,
All de gals I draw from over cross de way,
Wid my long-tail coat, mustache to de eye,
Dat's what dey like, boys—root hog or die.
New York gals, &c.

I'll go back to Alabama wid a head full of nollige,
And tell de folks dare I jis cum from college;
Dey'll take me for a lord, or somethin' else, I'm thinkin
I'se a mighty smart nigger, but I do my own drinkin'.
New York gals, &c.

ROOT HOG OR DIE, NO. 4.

I am de greatest little darkey on de top ob de earth,
New York is my home and de place ob my birth
I do ply upon de banjo, and dar I don't deny,
I'm bound to be a sport, boys—root hog or die.

CHORUS.

Now I'll tell all you, boys, what you'd better stop a doing,
Dat is a drinking lager beer, and give up tobacco chewing;
Now I'll tell all you boys, what you'd better stop a doing,
Dat is a drinking lager beer, and give up tobacco chewing.
Jog along.

De shanghai coats and de stub-toed boots,
Tight-legg'd pants, and all such fancy suits,
Big Byron collars and mustaches to de eye,
Dat's de way to sport, boys—root hog or die.
Now I'll tell you all, &c.

Now I'll tell you, one and all, dat I feel mighty proud,
When I have my banjo wid me, and gets into a crowd,
Dey do make a circle round me, and out dey do cry,
For to sing dis good old song, boys—root hog or die.
Now I'll tell you all, &c.

You may talk about your fiddles and de old tambo,
But they cannot be compared with de old banjo,
On it I'll end my song, and I'm not ashamed to deny
The title that I give it, boys, was—root hog or die.
Now I'll tell you all, &c.

TWENTY YEARS AGO.

I have wander'd by the village, Tom—I've sat beneath the tree,
Upon the school-house playing-ground which shelter'd you and me;
But none are left to greet me, Tom, and few are left to know
That play'd with us upon the green just Twenty Years Ago.

The grass is just as green, dear Tom, bare-footed boys at play
Are sporting just as we were then, with spirits just as gay;
But master sleeps upon the hill, all coated o'er with snow,
That afforded us a sliding-place just Twenty Years Ago.

The old school-house is alter'd some, the benches are replaced
By new ones, very like the same our penknives had defaced;
But the same old bricks are in the wall, the bell swings to and fro,
The music just the same, dear Tom, 'twas Twenty Years Ago.

The boys are playing some old game, beneath that same old tree,
I do forget the name just now—you have play'd the same with me;
On that same spot 'twas play'd with knives, by throwing so and so,
The leaders had a task to do there Twenty Years Ago.

The river is running just as still—the willows on its side
Are larger than they were, dear Tom, the stream appears less wide;
The grape-vine swing is ruin'd now, where once we play'd the beau,
And swung our sweethearts, pretty girls, just Twenty Years Ago.

The spring that bubbled 'neath the hill, close by the spreading beach,
Is very high--'twas once so low that we could almost reach,
But in kneeling down to get a drink, dear Tom, I started so,
To see how sadly I am changed since Twenty Years Ago.

Down by the spring upon an elm you know I cut your name—
Your sweetheart is just beneath it Tom—and you did mine the same,
Some heartless wretch has peel'd the bark--'twas dying sure but slow,
Just as the one whose name you cut did Twenty Years Ago.

My lids have long been dry, dear Tom, but tears come in my eyes,
I thought of her I loved so well—those early broken ties;
I visited the old churchyard, and took some flowers to strew
Upon the graves of those we loved some Twenty Years Ago.

Some are in the churchyard laid, some sleep beneath the sea,
But few are left of our old class, excepting you and me:
But when our time shall come, dear Tom, and we are call'd to go,

I hope they'll lay us were we play'd just Twenty Years Ago.

STAR SPANGLED BANNER.

Oh! say, can you see by the dawn's early light,
What so proudly we hail'd at the twilight's last gleaming;
Whose broad stripes and bright stars through the perilous fight,
O'er the ramparts we watch'd, were so gallantly streaming
And the rocket's red glare, the bombs bursting in air,
Gave proof through the night that our flag was still there,
Oh! say, does the star-spangled banner still wave,
O'er the land of the free, and the home of the brave?

On the shore, dimly seen through the mist of the deep,
Where the foe's haughty host in dread silence reposes,
What is that, which the breeze o'er the towering steep,
As it fitfully blows, half conceal'd, half discloses?
Now it catches the gleam of the morning's first beam,
In full glory reflected now shines on the stream;
'Tis the star-spangled banner, Oh! long may it wave,
O'er the land of the free, and the home of the brave.

And where is the band who so vauntingly swore
That the havoc of war, and the battle's confusion,
A home and a country should leave us no more?
Their blood has wash'd out their foul footstep's pollution.
No refuge could save the hireling and slave,
From the terror of flight or the gloom of the grave;
And the star-spangled banner in triumph doth wave,
O'er the land of the free, and the home of the brave.

Oh! thus be it ever when freemen shall stand
Between their loved home and war's desolation;
Bless'd with victory and peace may the Heaven-rescued land
Praise the power that hath made and preserved us a nation.
Then conquer we must, when our cause it is just,
And this be our motto--"In God is our trust!"
And the star-spangled banner in triumph shall wave,
O'er the land of the free, and the home of the brave.

SONG OF THE SEXTON.

Oh, the sights that I see as I ply my lone trade,
In the moldering dust that a cent'ry hath made,
Where the coffin-worm doth creep.
I began long ago, when my life was still green,
And my mattock and spade have been active, I ween,
To fashion the grave so deep.
Ho! I laugh as I dig, for they all seek my aid,
To provide them a home with my mattock and spade.

The rich man hath pass'd me with towering head,
But I sang o'er his grave when the scorner was dead,
And laugh'd as I shovel'd the mold.
The hungry and wretched ne'er enter'd his door,
His heart never bled for the wrongs of the poor,
For the proud man well loved his gold.
Ho! I laugh'd as I dug, for they wanted my aid,
To provide him a home with my mattock and spade.

I saw a young man in the fresh bloom of life,
As he came to the church with a trembling young wife,
Lift against me the finger of scorn.
Oh, the revel was joyous, the dance lasted long;
But the shriek of the widow soon banish'd the song—
The young man died ere the morn!
Ho! I laugh'd as I dug, when they came for my aid,
To provide him a home with my mattock and spade.

I saw a fair child bend her beautiful head,
And cull the lone flowers that bloom o'er the dead,
To form a pure simple wreath.
The crimson of hectic suffused her pale face;
In her eyes fearful lustre I trembled to trace,
The herald of early death.
But I pray that ere then, the deep home I have made,
May close over *me*, and my mattock and spade.

UNCLE SAM'S FARM.

Of all the mighty nations, in the East or in the West,
Oh! this glorious Yankee nation is the greatest and the best.
We have room for all creation, and our banner is unfurl'd,
Here is a general invitation to the people of the world.

Chorus.—Come along, come along—make no delay,
Come from every nation, come from every way;
Our land is broad enough—don't be alarmed,
For Uncle Sam is rich enough to give us all a farm.

St. Lawrence marks our northern line, as fast her waters flow,
And the Rio Grande our southern bound, way down to Mexico;
From the great Atlantic ocean, where the sun begins to dawn,
Leaps across the Rocky Mountains, away to Oregon.

Chorus.—Come along, come along, &c.

The South may raise the cotton, and the West the corn and pork,
New England manufactories shall do up the finer work;
For the deep and flowing waterfalls that course along our hills,
Are just the thing for washing sheep and driving cotton mills.

Chorus.—Come along, come along, &c.

Our fathers gave us liberty, but little did they dream,
The grand results that flow along this mighty age of steam;
For our mountains, lakes, and rivers are all a blaze of fire,
And we send our news by lightning on the telegraphic wire.

Chorus.—Come along, come along, &c.

Yes, we are bound to beat the nations, for our motto's go-ahead,
And we'll tell the foreign paupers that our people are well-fed;
For the nations must remember that Uncle Sam is not a fool,
For the people do the voting, and the children go to school.

Chorus.—Come along, come along, &c.

WAIT FOR THE WAGON.

Will you come with me, my Phillis, dear, to yon blue mountain free,
Where the blossoms smell the sweetest, come rove along with me.
It's every Sunday morning, when I am by your side,
We'll jump into the wagon, and all take a ride.

CHORUS.

Wait for the wagon,
Wait for the wagon,
Wait for the wagon,
And we'll all take a ride.

Where the river runs like silver, and the birds they sing so sweet,
I have a cabin, Phillis, and something good to eat.
Come listen to my story, it will relieve my heart,
So jump into the wagon, and off we will start.

Wait for the wagon, &c.

Do you believe, my Phillis, dear, old Mike with all his wealth,
Can make you half so happy, as I with youth and health?
We'll have a little farm, a horse, a pig, and cow,
And you will mind the dairy, while I do guide the plow.

Wait for the wagon, &c.

Your lips are red as poppies, your hair so slick and neat,
All braided up with dahlias, and hollyhocks so sweet,
It's every Sunday morning, when I am by your side,
We'll jump into the wagon, and all take a ride.

Wait for the wagon, &c.

Together on life's journey, we'll travel till we stop,
And if we have no trouble, we'll reach the happy top.
Then come with me, sweet Phillis, my dear, my lovely bride,
We'll jump into the wagon, and all take a ride.

Wait for the wagon, &c.

THE OLD FARM-HOUSE.

Oh, the old farm-house, down beside the valley stream,
Where in childhood so oft I have play'd,
Ere sorrow had clouded my heart's early dream,
Or life's purest joys had decay'd;
How well I remember the vine-cover'd roof,
And the rose-bushes clustering nigh,
And the tall, stately poplar-trees standing aloof,
Whose tops seem'd to reach to the sky,
Oh! the old farm-house, my childhood's happy home.

Oh, the old farm-house, how I've sported round its hearth
With my sisters and brothers so dear;
How oft has it rung with our innocent mirth,
And hallow'd our soft evening-prayer;
But the old farm-house now is bowing to decay,
Its stones like dead friends lie apart;
But its dear, cherish'd image shall ne'er fade away
From affection's domain in my heart.
Oh! the old farm-house, my childhood's happy home.

THE SWORD OF BUNKER HILL.

He lay upon his dying bed,
His eye was growing dim,
When with a feeble voice he call'd,
His weeping son to him:
"Weep not, my boy," the veteran said,
"I bow to Heaven's high will,
But quickly from yon antlers bring,
The sword of Bunker hill."
But quickly from yon antlers bring,
The sword of Bunker hill."

The sword was brought, the soldier's eye
Lit with a sudden flame;
And as he grasp'd the ancient blade,
He murmur'd Warren's name;
Then said, "My boy, I leave you gold,
But what is richer still,
I leave you, mark me, mark me, now,
The sword of Bunker Hill.
I leave you, mark me, mark me, now,
The sword of Bunker Hill.

"Twas on that dread, immortal day,
I dared the Briton's band,
A captain raised this blade on me,
I tore it from his hand;
And while the glorious battle raged,
It lighten'd freedom's will,
For, boy, the God of Freedom bless'd
The sword of Bunker Hill.
For, boy, the God of Freedom bless'd
The sword of Bunker Hill.

"Oh! keep the sword," his accents broke,
A smile, and he was dead;
But his wrinkled hand still grasp'd the blade,
Upon that dying bed.

The son remains, the sword remains,
Its glory growing still,
And twenty millions bless the sire
And sword of Bunker Hill.
And twenty millions bless the sire
And sword of Bunker Hill.

A NATIONAL SONG.

God of the Free! to thee we look,
As look'd our sires in days of old,
When on thy breath invoked by prayer,
Their banner for the Right unroll'd.

That glorious banner still is ours;
Our falchions like their own shall start,
When Freedom's sent'nel-trumpet calls,
To find the impious tyrant's heart.

Their sacred homesteads still we own,
And still the wave of Plymouth rolls
The hymn of Justice, Labor, Right,
And blest Religion in our souls.

Their mighty mission was not left
By them in vain for us, for we,
Heirs of a continent, are yet
Subduing mountain, vale, and sea.

How proudly on our march we go,
With Washington's own flag unfurl'd;
The blood of all the world is here,
And he who strikes us, strikes the world!

Then wave thine oaken bough, O North!
O South! exulting lift thy palms;
And in our Union's heritage
Together sing the Nation's psalms.

BELLE BRANDON.

'Neath a tree by the margin of a woodland,
Whose spreading leafy boughs sweep the ground,
With a path leading thither o'er the prairie,
Where silence hung her night garb around;
Where oft I have wander'd in the evening,
When the summer winds were fragrant on the lea,
There I saw the little beauty Belle Brandon,
And we met 'neath the old arbor tree.

REPEAT.

There I saw the little beauty, Belle Brandon,
And we met 'neath the old arbor tree.

Belle Brandon was a birdling of the mountain,
In freedom she sported on the lea,
And they said the life current of the red man
Tinged her veins, from a far distant sea.
And she loved her humble dwelling on the prairie,
And her guileless happy heart clung to me,
And I loved the little beauty, Belle Brandon,
And we both loved the old arbor tree.
Repeat.—And I loved the little beauty, &c.

On the trunk of an aged tree I carved them,
And our names on the sturdy oak remain,
But I now repair in sorrow to its shelter,
And murmur to the wild winds my pain.
And I sat there in solitude repining,
For the beauty dream night brought to me,
Death has wed the little beauty, Belle Brandon,
And she sleeps 'neath the old arbor tree.
Repeat.—Death has wed the little beauty, &c.

THE DYING CALIFORNIAN.

Lay up nearer, brother, nearer, for my limbs are growing cold,
And thy presence seemeth dearer when thy arms around me fold
I am dying, brother, dying, soon you'll miss me in your berth,
And my form will soon be lying 'neath the ocean's briny surf.

Hearken to me, brother, hearken, I have something I would say,
Ere this vail my vision darken, and I go from hence away;
I am going, surely going, but my hopes in God are strong,
I am willing, brother, knowing that He doeth nothing wrong.

Tell my father when you greet him, that in death I pray'd for him,
Pray'd that I might one day meet him, in a world that's free from sin;
Tell my mother, God assist her, now that she is growing old,
Tell, her son would glad have kiss'd her, when his lips grew pale and
cold.

Hearken to me—catch each whisper, 'tis my wife I speak of now.
Tell, oh, tell her, how I miss'd her, when the fever burnt my brow:
Hearken to me, closely listen, don't forget a single word,
That in death my eyes did glisten when the tears her memory stirr'd.

Tell her then to kiss my children, like the kiss I last impress'd,
Hold them fast as last I held them, fold'd closely to my breast;
Give them early to their Maker, putting all their trust in God,
And He will never forsake her—He has said so in His word.

O my childern, Heaven bless them! they were all my life to me;
Would I could once more caress them, ere I sink beneath the sea;
'Twas for them I cross'd the ocean—what my hopes were I'll not tell,
But they have gain'd an orphan's portion—yet He doeth all things well.

Tell my sisters I remember every kindly parting word,
And my heart has been kept tender by the thoughts their memory stirr'd;
Tell them I never reach'd the haven where I sought the precious dust,
But I've gain'd a port call'd heaven, where the gold doth never rust.

Urge them to secure an entrance, for they will find their brother there,
Faith in Jesus and repentance will secure for them a share;
Hark! I hear my Saviour calling--'tis I know his voice so well,
When I'm gone, oh, don't be weeping, brother, hear my last farewell!

I WANT TO GO HOME.

I want to go home,
For never a place did I see,
Wherever I roam, far away and alone,
So dear as my own Tennessee.
But now I am far away,
To my home I must go soon,
I want to go back to hunt for the deer track,
And watch for the possum and coon.

CHORUS.

I want to go home,
For never a place did I see,
Wherever I roam far away and alone,
So dear as my own Tennessee.

I want to go where
The sugar cane's growing so green,
For many a day have I wandered away,
To watch the old mill by the stream.
And when the night had come,
And the darkey's work was done,
We've gathered around, for a dance on the green
By the sound of the old Tamborine.

But now I am far away,
And lonely and sad is my lot,
I never can rest till my journey is past,
And I again seek my old cot.
From my childhood's happy home,
I never more will roam.
I will take by my side, my young Tennessee bride
And live ever happy at home.

BOLD PRIVATEER.

It's oh! my dearest Polly, you and I must part,
I am going across the seas, love, I give to you my heart,
My ship she lies in waiting, so fare thee well, my dear,
I am just a going on board of the Bold Privateer.

But oh, my dearest Johnny, great dangers have been cross'd,
And many a sweet life by the seas has been lost;
You had better stop at home with the girl that loves you dear,
Than to venture your life on the Bold Privateer.

When the wars are over, may heaven spare my life,
Then soon I will come back to my sweet, loving wife.
Then soon I will get married to charming Polly dear,
And forever bid adieu to the Bold Privateer.

Oh! my dearest Polly, your friends do me dislike,
Besides you have two brothers who'd quickly take my life.
Come, change your ring with me, my dear, come change your
ring with me,
And that shall be our token when I am on the sea.

HEATHER DALE.

In a peaceful little valley,
Where the violets grow,
There I used to wander daily,
Watching at the brooklet's flow;
Not a spot I loved so dearly
As this fragrant vale,
And I never shall forget it,
Lovely little Heather Dale!

Chorus. —Oh, how I always loved to,
With my sister Nell,
Roam in days of youthful pleasure
In that little Heather Dale.

There I've heard the little songsters
Sing their songs of glee,
Skipping from the waving tree-tops,
'Twas a lovely sight to me;
Fragrance from the little flowers
Fill'd each gentle gale,
As they in their course came playing
Through the little Heather Dale.

Chorus. —Oh, how I always loved to, &c.

Now those childhood's days have fleeted,
And no more I'll roam,
In that quiet little valley
Near my old sequester'd home;
But I always shall remember
Where I used to trail,
Through that lone and silent valley,
My own little Heather Dale.

Chorus. —Oh, how I always loved to &c.

THE MARSEILLES HYMN.

Ye sons of Freedom, awake to glory!
Hark! hark! what myriads bid you rise?
Your children, wives, and grandsires hoary,
Behold their tears and hear their cries.
Shall hateful tyrants, mischiefs breeding,
With hireling hosts, a ruffian band,
Affright and desolate the land,
While peace and liberty lie bleeding?
To arms! to arms! ye brave!
The avenging sword unsheath:
March on! march on! all hearts resolved
On victory or death.

Now, now, the dangerous storm is rolling,
Which treacherous kings confederate raise;
The dogs of war, let loose, are howling,
And lo! our fields and cities blaze;
And shall we basely view the ruin,
While lawless force, with guilty stride,
Spreads desolation far and wide,
With crimes and blood his hands embruing?
To arms! to arms! ye brave, &c.

With luxury and pride surrounded,
The vile, insatiate despots dare,
(Their thirst of power and gold unbounded),
To mete and vend the light and air.
Like beasts of burden would they load us,
Like gods would bid their slaves adore
But man is man, and who is more?
Then shall they longer lash and goad us?
To arms! to arms! ye brave, &c.

O Liberty! can man resign thee,
Once having felt thy generous flame?
Can dungeons, bolts, or bars confine thee?
Or whips thy noble spirit tame?
Too long the world has wept, bewailing
That falsehood's dagger tyrants wield,

But freedom is our sword and shield,
And all their arts are unavailing.
To arms! to arms! ye brave, &c.

TWINKLING STARS.

Twinkling stars are laughing, love,
Laughing on you and me,
While your bright eyes look in mine,
Peeping stars they seem to be;
Troubles come and go, love,
Brightest scenes must leave our sight,
But the star of hope, love,
Shines with radiant beams to-night.

CHORUS.

Twinkling stars are laughing, love,
Laughing on you and me,
While your bright eyes look in mine,
Peeping stars they seem to be.

Golden beams are shining, love,
Shining on you to bless,
Like the queen of night, you fill
Darkest space with loveliness.
Silver stars how bright, love,
Mother moon in thronely might,
Gaze on us to bless, love,
Purest vows here made to-night.
Chorus.—Twinkling stars, &c.

SHELLS OF THE OCEAN.

One summer eve, with pensive thought,
I wandered on the sea-beat shore,
Where oft, in heedless infant sport,
I gathered shells in days before.
I gathered shells, &c.

The plashing waves, like music fell,
Responsive to my fancy wild,
A dream came o'er me like a spell,
I thought I was again a child.
A dream came o'er me like a spell,
A dream came o'er me like a spell,
I thought I was again a child.

I stooped upon the pebbly strand,
To cull the toys that 'round me lay,
But as I took them in my hand,
I threw them one by one away.
I threw them, &c.

"Oh, thus," I said, "in every stage,
By toys our fancy is beguiled,
We gather shells from youth to age,
And then we leave them like a child."
We gathere shells, &c.

OLD DOG TRAY.

The morn of life is past, and evening comes at last,
It brings me a dream of a once happy day,
Of many forms I've seen, upon the village green,
Sporting with my old Dog Tray.

CHORUS.

Old Dog Tray's ever faithful,
Grief can not drive him away
He's gentle, he is kind, I'll never, never find,
A better friend than old Dog Tray,

The forms I call'd my own, have vanish'd one by one,
The loved ones, the dear ones, have all pass'd away;
Their happy smiles have flown, their gentle voices gone,
I have nothing left but old Dog Tray.

Old Dog Tray's ever faithful,
Grief can never drive him away,
He's gentle, he is kind; I'll never, never find,
A better friend than old Dog Tray.

When thoughts recall the past, his eyes are on me cast,
I know that he feels what my breaking heart would say,
Although he can not speak, I'll vainly, vainly seek,
A better friend than old Dog Tray.

Old Dog Tray's ever faithful,
Grief can not drive him away,
He's gentle, he is kind; I'll never, never find.
A better friend than old Dog Tray.

RED, WHITE, AND BLUE.

Oh Columbia, the gem of the ocean,
The home of the brave and the free,
The shrine of each patriot's devotion,
A world offers homage to thee.
Thy mandates make heroes assemble,
When liberty's form stands in view,
Thy banners make tyranny tremble,
When borne by the red, white, and blue.
When borne by the red, white, and blue,
When borne by the red, white, and blue,
Thy banners make tyranny tremble,
When borne by the red, white, and blue.

When war waged its wide desolation,
And threaten'd our land to deform,
The ark then of freedom's foundation,
Columbia rode safe through the storm.
With her garland of victory o'er her,
When so proudly she bore her bold crew,
With her flag proudly floating before her,
The boast of the red, white, and blue.
The boast of, &c.

The wine cup, the wine cup bring hither,
And fill you it up to the brim,
May the wreath they have won never wither
Nor the star of their glory grow dim,
May the service united ne'er sever,
And hold to their colors so true,
The army and navy forever,
Three cheers for the red, white, and blue.
Three cheers for, &c.

THE ROCK OF LIBERTY.

Oh! the firm old rock, the wave-worn rock,
That braved the blast and the billow's shock;
It was born with time on a barren shore,
And it laugh'd with scorn at the ocean's roar.
'Twas here that first the Pilgrim band,
Came weary up to the foaming strand;
And the tree they rear'd in the days gone by,
It lives, it lives, it lives, and ne'er shall die.

Thou stern old rock in the ages past,
Thy brow was bleach'd by the warring blast;
But thy wintry toil with the wave is o'er,
And the billows beat thy base no more.
Yet countless as thy sands, old rock,
Are the hardy sons of the Pilgrim stock;
And the tree they rear'd in the days gone by,
It lives, it lives, it lives, and ne'er shall die.

Then rest, old rock, on the sea-beat shore,
Our sires are lull'd by the breaker's roar;
'Twas here that first their hymns were heard
O'er the startled cry of the ocean bird.
'Twas here they lived, 'twas here they died,
Their forms repose on the green hill-side;
And the tree they rear'd in the days gone by,
It lives, it lives, it lives, and ne'er shall die.

OUR MARY ANN.

Oh, fare you well, my own Mary Ann,
Fare you well for a while;
The ship is ready, and the wind is fair,
And I am bound for the sea, Mary Ann.

Oh, didn't you see your *turtile* dove,
A sittin' on yonder pile,
Lamenting the loss of his own true love,
And so am I for my Mary Ann.

Oh, fare you well, &c.

A lobster in a lobster pot,
A blue fish in a brook,
May suffer some—but you know not,
What I do feel for my Mary Ann.

Oh, fare you well, &c.

The pride of all the produce ground,
The dinner kitchen-garden fruit,
Is *pnmpkins* some, but can't compare,
The love I bear for my Mary Ann.
Oh, fare you well, &c.

EVENING STAR.

Beautiful star in heaven so bright,
Softly falls thy silver light,
As thou movest from earth afar,
Star of the evening—beautiful star.
Beautiful star, beautiful star,
Star of the evening,
Beautiful, beautiful star.

In fancy's eyes thou seemst to say,
Follow me, come from earth away;
Upward they spirit's pinions try,
To realms of love beyond the sky.
Beautiful star, &c.

Shine on! O star of love divine,
And may our souls around thee twine,
As thou movest from earth afar,
Star of the twilight—beautiful star.
Beautiful star, &c.

THE AGE OF PROGRESS.

The age of giant progress,
Americans all hail!
The land, all interwoven
With telegraph and rail;
No sluggish chains shall bind us,
No tardiness delay;
The morning light is breaking (waking)
O'er our destiny.

The age of trained lightning,
"Dispatching" human thought;
What wondrous revolution
The scheme of Morse hath wrought!
No time, no space can hinder
The quick, electric fire;
Intelligence is flashing (dashing)
O'er the magic wire.

The age of grand conceptions,
The "cable of the deep!"
It "snapp'd," but we will mend it,
We have no time to weep.
The great Pacific Railroad!
'Twill not be long before
The railroad cars are flying (hieing)
From the golden shore.

The age of priceless knowledge,
The scholar's jubilee!
The land all dotted over
With institutions free.
Our public schools! Oh, hail them!
They offer treasures cheap:
The boys and girls are scaling (hailing)
Science's rugged steep.

GLAD TO GET HOME.

Oh, how glad to get home,
For far I've wander'd,
Joyful, joyful I come,
Dear home, to thee!
Fond ones welcome me here,
Loved ones are near me;
Voices float on my ear,
Sweet, sweet to me.

CHORUS.

Dear friends that are round me, haste with looks delighted,
Days long vanish'd and gone, come to my heart.
Dear home of my childhood, once again united,
Never, never again from thee I'll part.

Father, in the warm grasp
I feel thy welcome,
Oh, from love's tender clasp
Ne'er let me fly;
Mother, fondly again
Thou dost enfold me;
Tears I can not restrain
Burst from mine eye.
Chorus. — Dear friends that are round me, &c.

Brother, still is thy brow
Noble as ever,
As I look on thee now,
How swells my heart!
Sister, gentle and kind,
Close to me clinging;
Now in love we are twined
No more to part.
Chorus. — Dear friends that are round me, &c.

BLIND ORPHAN BOY'S LAMENT.

"They tell me that my mother's sleeping
In the church-yard far away,
That she knows not I am weeping—
Weeping all the live long day.

"They tell me that my father's lying
In the dark grave by her side;
That I'm left on life's rough billow
With no earthly friend or guide.

"When the wild woods echo loudly,
And the merry songsters sing,
When the winds are hurrying past me
With sweet music on their wings,

"Methinks I hear my mother calling,
And her grave I long to find;
But there's no one here to lead me,
For the orphan boy is blind."

He now sleeps within that church-yard
Where he ofttimes long'd to be;
Angels bore his soul to heaven,
Now the poor blind boy can see.

THE LAKE-SIDE SHORE.

Summer's breath is lightly falling
On the silent waters blue,
And the moonbeams bright are sporting
With the drops of glittering dew;
Hark! away upon the waters
There's a sound of dipping oar,
And a boat-song loudly chanted,
Echoes down the lake-side shore.

Now the night-bird's song comes floating
Sweetly down the midnight air,
Waking all the depths, to listen
To the birds that thus should dare
To break the weird and solemn stillness,
That had reign'd so long before,
In the wood, and mead, and valley,
On the silent lake-side shore.

Now the song comes swelling bolder,
And the boatman's chant is heard,
Louder o'er the distant waters,
As it would outvie the bird;
But each song at last is finish'd,
And the bird to rest once more,
Leaves no sound to break the quiet
Of the happy lake-side shore.

Who can say there is no pleasure
Thus to walk the night alone,
Listening to the night-bird's music,
Or the boatman's solemn tone?
Where is there a spot more lovely,
Where the vail of night hangs o'er?
Where another place more lovely
Than this silent lake-side shore?

THE TEMPEST.

We were crowded in the cabin,
Not a soul would dare to sleep,
It was midnight on the waters,
And the storm was o'er the deep
'Tis a fearful thing in winter
To be shatter'd by the blast,
And to hear the trumpet thunder,
"Cut away the mast!"

We shudder'd there in silence,
For the stoutest held his breath,
While the hungry sea was roaring,
And the breakers talk'd with death;
Sad thus we sat in silence,
All busy with our prayers,
"We're lost!" the captain shouted,
As he stagger'd down the stairs.

But his little daughter whisper'd.
As she took the icy hand,
"Is not God upon the waters,
Just the same as on the land?"
Then we kiss'd the little maiden,
And we spake of better cheer,
As we anchor'd safe in harbor,
Where the sun was shining clear.

Chorus.—And a shout rose loud and joyous,
As we grasp'd the friendly hand,
God is on the waters,
Just the same as on the land.

E PLURIBUS UNUM.

Copied by permission of PETERS & SONS, Fourth St. Cincinnati O owners of the
copyright.

Though many and bright are the stars that appear
In the flag of our country unfurl'd;
And the stripes that are swelling in majesty there,
Like a rainbow adorning the world;
Their lights are unsullied as those in the sky,
By a deed that our fathers have done,
And they're leagued in as true and as holy a tie,
In their motto of "Many in one."

From the hour when those patriots fearlessly flung
That banner of star-light abroad,
Ever true to themselves, to that motto they clung
As they clung to the promise of God;
By the bayonet traced at the midnight of war,
On the fields where our glory was won,
Oh! perish the hand, or the heart that would mar
Our motto of "Many in one."

'Mid the smoke of the contest, the cannon's deep roar.
How oft it hath gather'd renown;
While those stars were reflected in rivers of gore,
When the cross and the lion went down.
And though few were their lights in the gloom of that hour,
Yet the hearts that were striking below,
Had God for their bulwark, and truth for their power,
And they stopp'd not to number the foe.

We are many in one where there glitters a star
In the blue of the heavens above,
And tyrants shall quail 'mid their dungeons afar,
When they gaze on our motto of love.
It shall gleam o'er the sea 'mid the bolts of the storm,
O'er the tempest, and battle, and wreck,
And flame where our guns with their thunder grow warm,
'Neath the blood on the slippery deck.

Then up with our flag, let it stream on the air,
Though our fathers are cold in their graves;

They had hands that could strike, they had souls that could dare,
And their sons were not born to be slaves.
Up, up with our banner where'er it may call,
Our millions shall rally around,
A nation of freemen that moment shall fall,
When its stars shall be trail'd on the ground.

A GOOD TIME COMING.

There is a good time coming, boys,
A good time coming;
There's a good time coming, boys,
Wait a little longer;
We may not live to see the day,
But earth shall glisten in the ray
Of the good time coming;
Cannon-balls may aid the truth,
But thought's a weapon stronger;
We'll win our battles by its aid,
Wait a little longer.
There's a good time coming, boys,
A good time coming,
There's a good time coming, boys.
Wait a little longer.

There's a good time coming, boys,
A good time coming;
There's a good time coming, boys,
Wait a little longer;
The pen shall supersede the sword,
And right, not might, shall be the lord,
In the good time comidg;
Worth, not birth, shall rule mankind,
And be acknowledged stronger,
The proper impulse has been given,
Wait a little longer.
There's a good time coming, boys,
A good time coming,
There's a good time coming, boys,
Wait a little longer.

THE HILLS OF NEW ENGLAND.

The hills of New England, how proudly they rise,
In their wildness of grandeur to blend with the skies,
With their far azure outline, and tall, ancient trees,
New England, my country, I love thee for these.

The vales of New England, that cradle her streams,
And smile in their beauty like land in our dreams;
All sunny with beauty, embosom'd in ease.
New England, my country, I love thee for these.

The woods of New England, still verdant and high,
Though rock'd by the tempest of ages gone by;
Romance dims their arches, and speaks in the breeze,
New England, my country, I love thee for these.

The streams of New England, that roar as they go,
Or seem in their wildness but dreaming to flow;
Oh! bright gilds the sunbeam their march to the seas,
New England, my country, I love thee for these.

The homes of New England, free, fortuned, and fair;
Oh, many a heart treasures its seraphim there,
E'en more than thy mountains or streamlets they please,
New England, my country, I love thee for these.

God shield thee, New England, dear land of my birth,
And thy children that wander afar on the earth;
Thou still art my country, where'er I am cast, —
Take thou to thy bosom my ashes at last.

THE OLD FOLKS WE LOVED LONG AGO.

Battling with life,
'Mid care and strife,
The daily toils in hope I undergo;
Yet mem'ry will wander,
Fonder oh, fonder,
To the dear old folks I loved long ago.

Long years have gone
Since in the morn
Of life I heard the river's gentle flow;
And oft mem'ry lingers,
As point time's fingers,
To the dear old folks I loved long ago.

Dell, hill, and tree,
Flower, bird, and bee,
All as of yore, make music sweet and low,
And, though on earth riven,
I hope to meet in heaven
The dear old folks I loved long ago.

Then up, my soul,
Strive for the goal,
Oh, linger not to weep and wail in woe;
For far in yon azure blue
Methinks I yet may know
The dear old folks I loved long ago.

Lector House believes that a society develops through a two-fold approach of continuous learning and adaptation, which is derived from the study of classic literary works spread across the historic timeline of literature records. Therefore, we aim at reviving, repairing and redeveloping all those inaccessible or damaged but historically as well as culturally important literature across subjects so that the future generations may have an opportunity to study and learn from past works to embark upon a journey of creating a better future.

This book is a result of an effort made by Lector House towards making a contribution to the preservation and repair of original ancient works which might hold historical significance to the approach of continuous learning across subjects.

HAPPY READING & LEARNING!

LECTOR HOUSE LLP
E-MAIL: lectorpublishing@gmail.com